# ROALD DAHL

# MATILDA's JOKES

## FOR AWESOME KIDS

PUFFIN BOOKS

UK | USA | Canada | Ireland | Australia
India | New Zealand | South Africa

Puffin Books is part of the Penguin Random House group of companies
whose addresses can be found at global.penguinrandomhouse.com.

www.penguin.co.uk    www.puffin.co.uk    www.ladybird.co.uk

 Penguin
Random House
UK

First published 2019

001

Text design by Perfect Bound Ltd
Printed in Great Britain by Clays Ltd, Elcograf S.p.A.

A CIP catalogue record for this book is available from the British Library

ISBN: 978-0-241-42213-7

All correspondence to:
Puffin Books
Penguin Random House Children's
80 Strand, London WC2R 0RL

MIX
Paper from
responsible sources
FSC® C018179

Penguin Random House is committed to a
sustainable future for our business, our readers
and our planet. This book is made from Forest
Stewardship Council® certified paper.

# ROALD DAHL

# MATILDA's JOKES

## FOR AWESOME KIDS

PUFFIN

# WELCOME TO CRUNCHEM HALL

This is Matilda.

Matilda is five and a half years old and she is **EXTRAORDINARY**. By the age of three she had taught herself to read; by the age of four she was reading everything she could get her hands on; and by the time she started school she had read everything in her local library.

Matilda goes to school at Crunchem Hall. Her teacher, Miss Honey, thinks that she is a **GENIUS** and a **PHENOMENON**. But her headmistress, the horrid Miss Trunchbull, thinks that she is a **VIPER**, a **LITTLE BEAST** and a **GANGSTER**. (Miss Trunchbull is an awful person.)

School is not much fun for the boys and girls who live under Miss Trunchbull's reign of terror. This book contains jokes to brighten up **EVERY** hour of the school day, from taking the register to home time. There are hilarious history jokes, groan-worthy geography jokes and side-splitting science jokes for you to enjoy and to share with your friends.

Some of these jokes are **VERY CLEVER**, like Matilda, so if you don't get them, ask someone clever, like a teacher. (But not the **HORRENDOUS** Trunchbull. Keep well clear, is my advice.)

It's time to get ready – the school day is about to **BEGIN**!

# CONTENTS

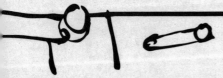

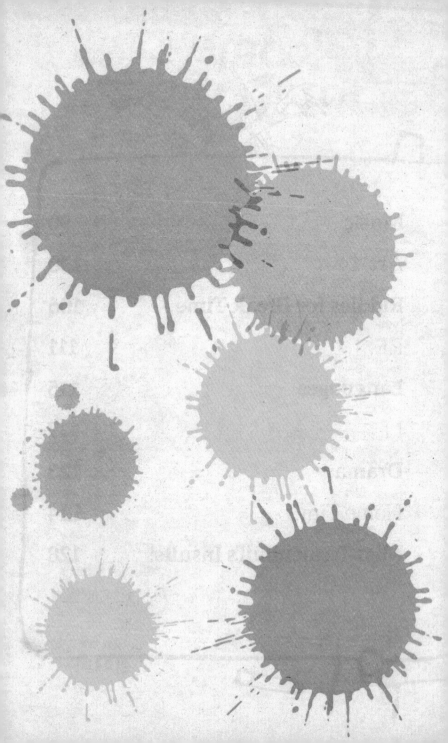

# Welcome to SCHOOL

I was really excited to be starting school. That is, until I met **THE TRUNCHBULL**...

How do **BEES** get to school?

On the **SCHOOL BUZZ.**

What do you do if you find a **GORILLA** sitting at your school desk?

Find **SOMEWHERE ELSE** to sit!

When are school uniforms **FIRE HAZARDS**?

When they're **BLAZERS.**

What do you do if your teacher **ROLLS HER EYES** at you?

**Pick them up and roll them back.**

What do you call a teacher with a banana in each ear? **NOTHING,** they can't hear you.

I'd tell you the joke about the blunt pencil …

**But it's POINTLESS.**

Did you hear the joke about the school roof?

**Never mind, it's OVER YOUR HEAD.**

Why was the **MARSUPIAL** hired to teach Year Three?

**He had the necessary koalafications.**

LAVENDER: Miss Honey, would you punish someone for something they hadn't done?

MISS HONEY: **Of course not!**

LAVENDER: Great, because I haven't done my homework.

Which fruit **NEVER PLAYS BY ITSELF** at break time?

A PEAR.

MISS TRUNCHBULL: You're late. You should have been here at nine o'clock.

LAVENDER: **Why? Did something happen?**

MISS TRUNCHBULL: You're *always* late.

LAVENDER: **Well, you keep ringing the bell before I get here.**

WILFRED: Sir, sir! Prudence keeps saying I'm a clock!
MR TRILBY: **Don't worry, she's just winding you up.**

What do you call a **TROLL** who gets perfect marks at school?

**An ogre-achiever.**

I'm sorry I'm late for school – we got a puncture. There was a **FORK** in the road.

What's the first thing a teacher does in the morning?

**WAKES UP.**

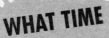**WHAT TIME** is it when Miss Trunchbull sits on your watch? **Time to get a NEW WATCH.**

What's the best thing to give a **TRAVEL-SICK** pupil on a school bus trip? **Plenty of room.**

BRUCE BOGTROTTER: **Miss, miss, I keep thinking I'm a dog!**

MISS PLIMSOLL: How long have you thought this?

BRUCE: **Ever since I was a puppy.**

Why do cats do badly at school? **THEY FUR-GET THINGS.**

Did you hear the joke about the teacher who swallowed a clock?

**It was time-consuming.**

What do you call ten teachers in a phone box?
**STUCK.**

What do snakes learn at school?
**To read and writhe.**

By the classroom blackboard, one piece of chalk said to the other,
**'I FEEL A BIT SQUEAKY.'**

The other piece of chalk said,
**'AAAARGH!
TALKING CHALK!'**

What did the pencil say to the rubber? **'TAKE ME TO YOUR RULER.'**

Why did the pupil take a ladder to school? **Because it was a HIGH SCHOOL.**

Why do **TOADSTOOLS** sit so close together in class? **They don't need mushroom.**

Why did Miss Trunchbull **RUN AROUND** her bed? **She wanted to catch up on her sleep.**

# Meet the
# TEACHERS

**OH GOODNESS,** these are some clever jokes to tease your teachers!

RUPERT: Miss, miss, I think I'm becoming a pencil!
MISS HONEY: **Yes, I can see your point.**

PRUDENCE: Miss, miss, I've got a strawberry growing out of my head!
MISS PLIMSOLL: **Go to the nurse and get some cream for it.**

Why did Mr Trilby wear **GLASSES**?
**To control his pupils.**

Why did Miss Honey wear sunglasses inside?
Because her class was **SO BRIGHT.**

PRUDENCE: **Miss, miss, will you still remember me in twenty years?**
MISS PLIMSOLL: Of course!
PRUDENCE: **Knock, knock.**
MISS PLIMSOLL: Who's there?
PRUDENCE: **See? You've forgotten me already!**

What's louder than an angry teacher?
**TWO ANGRY TEACHERS.**

MISS HONEY: Can anyone name two days of the week that begin with 'T'?
FRED: **Today and tomorrow.**

LAVENDER: **Miss, miss, I think I'm invisible!**
MISS PLIMSOLL: Who said that?

WILFRED: Sir, sir, I think I've lost my memory.
MR TRILBY: **When did this happen?**
WILFRED: When did what happen?

LAVENDER: Miss, miss, I keep seeing spinning insects!
MISS HONEY: **Don't worry, it's just a bug that's going round.**

Why did the girl **EAT** her homework?
Because her teacher said it was a piece of cake.

# TAKING THE REGISTER

Miss Honey always starts the day by taking the register. Can you guess the **NAMES** of her pupils?

What do you call a boy lying by the front door?
**MATT.**

Knock, knock.
**Who's there?**
Norma.
**Norma who?**
Normally I have a key!

What do you call a boy with '9 out of 10' written on his head? **MARK.**

What do you call a girl standing between two goalposts? **ANNETTE.**

What do you call a girl dressed from **HEAD TO TOE** in denim? **Jean.**

**Knock, knock.**
Who's there?
**Harry.**
Harry who?
**Harry up and let me in, I'm late for school!**

What do you call a boy with a nose like a duck? **BILL.**

What do you call a boy with a **SEAGULL** on his head? **Cliff.**

What do you call a pirate who gets **0 OUT OF 10** in a spelling test? **Wrong John Silver.**

Knock, knock.
**Who's there?**
Ash.
**Ash who?**
Bless you!

What do you call a boy with a **RABBIT** up his jumper? **Warren.**

What do you call a boy who walks all day? **MILES.**

What do you call a girl with a **TORTOISE** on her head?

**Shelley.**

What do you call a boy with a **BOULDER** on his head?

**Squashed.**

What do you call a girl with a **REEF** on her head?

**Coral.**

What do you call a boy with a **SPADE** on his head?

**Doug.**

What do you call a boy **WITHOUT** a spade on his head?

**DOUGLAS.**

What do you call a girl with a **STORM** on her head? **GAIL.**

What do you call a girl standing with **ONE LEG** on either side of a river?

**Bridget.**

What do you call a boy in a pile of leaves? **RUSSELL.**

What do you call a girl with a **FROG** on her head?

**Lily.**

# ENGLISH

I have no difficulty spelling: Mrs D, Mrs I, Mrs FFI, Mrs C, Mrs U, Mrs LTY!

## Spelling

How do you make a **WITCH** scratch?

**Take away the 'W'.**

What's a **WITCH'S** favourite subject at school?

**Spelling.**

What do you call a bird with no eyes?

**A BRD.**

The past, the present and the future walked into the classroom.

**It was TENSE.**

Have you ever had problems with existentialism?

**Only when I try to spell it.**

'How do you spell "serendipity"?'
**'S-E-R-I-N-N-D-I-P-P-I-T-T-E-E-E.'**

'That's not how the dictionary spells it.'
**'You didn't ask me how the dictionary spells it.'**

How do you scramble eggs?

**G-e-s-g.**

What is the scariest letter?

**S. It makes cream scream!**

'How do you spell "wrong"?'
**'R-O-N-G.'**
'That's wrong.'
**'That's what you asked for, isn't it?'**

Why do **FISH** take a really long time to learn the **ALPHABET**?

**They spend most of their time at C.**

'Give me a sentence starting with "I".'
**'I is . . .'**
'No, you must always say, "I am."'
**'OK, then: "I am the ninth letter of the alphabet."'**

# Puns

What's the difference between an iceberg and a clothes brush?
**One crushes BOATS and the other brushes COATS.**

Can February March?
**NO, BUT APRIL MAY!**

What's the difference between a **UNICORN** and a field of carrots?
**One's a funny beast, the other's a BUNNY FEAST.**

# Limericks

A gentleman dining at Crewe
**Found a rather large mouse in his stew.**
Cried the waiter, 'Don't shout
**And wave it about**
Or the rest will be wanting one too.'

The thing we all ask about Jenny
**Is, 'Surely there cannot be many**
Young girls in the place
**With so lovely a face?'**
The answer to that is, 'Not any!'

Matilda
wrote
this!

There was a young girl called Amanda
**Whose headmistress just couldn't stand 'er.**
The poor lass was swung
**By the pigtails and flung**
And no one knew WHERE that'd land her.

There once was a writer called Roald
**Whose books were a sight to behold.**
From witches to foxes,
**He ticked all the boxes,**
The very best tales ever told.

# THE SCHOOL LIBRARY

I **LOVE** the library! Here's Mrs Phelps with some **LOVELY** library jokes...

What is the tallest room in any school?
**The library. It has so many stories!**

'How many **BOOKS** have you read in your lifetime?'
**'I don't know yet, I'm still alive!'**

What do librarians take when they go fishing?
**BOOKWORMS.**

Today the librarian learned that words can be **HURTFUL**.

**She dropped a dictionary on her foot.**

What's a rabbit's **FAVOURITE** book? One with a hoppy ending.

What's a chicken's favourite book? **CLUCKLEBERRY FINN.**

# Fairy Tales

I started out by reading the entire children's section. **HANS CHRISTIAN ANDERSEN** and the **BROTHERS GRIMM** were my favourites. Do you recognize any of these characters?

Why does **PETER PAN** always fly?

Because he can Never-Never Land.

Why did **LITTLE BO-PEEP** lose her sheep?

She had a crook with her.

What's a **MERMAID'S** favourite book?

One with fairy tails.

What do you say to a **REALLY COOL** dragon?

'You're a legend!'

Why would **SNOW WHITE** make a great teacher?

**She's the fairest in the land.**

Where did **GOLDILOCKS** fall asleep?

**At the house of the three bores.**

Why do you never find a hamster librarian?

**They have NO TALES.**

Why did Old Mother Hubbard shriek?

**She found a SKELETON in the cupboard.**

# BOOK TITLES

*Never Make a Mermaid Angry*
by Sheila Tack

The Sharks Are Coming

by B. Warned

**Giant Rodents**

by
E. Norm
Ouse

**Potty Training**
by Enid A. Wee

**An A to Z of Letters**   by Alf A. Bet

'WE DON'T HOLD with book-reading,' Mr Wormwood said. 'You can't make a living from sitting on your fanny and reading STORY-BOOKS.'

SIMPLE MATHS by Ivor Nansa

Get Rich Quick by Robin Banks

Life on the Ocean Waves

by Eva Lot

My South Pole Adventure by Anne Tarctic

The Worst Adventure in the World

by Hellen Back

# MATHS

I can do lots of **SUMS** in my head but these maths jokes make me laugh out loud!

Why was the **MATHS** book **SAD**? It was full of problems.

What did the zero say to the eight? 'Nice belt.'

What's the quickest way to **DOUBLE YOUR MONEY**? Fold it in half.

Why is **6** afraid of **7**?
Because **7 8 9.**

What do you call a mother who is not very tall?
**A minimum.**

What do you call a mother who is very tall?
A **MAXIMUM.**

'If I have **FIVE** apples in one hand and **SIX** apples in the other, what would I have?'
'Big hands, sir.'

There's a fine line between a numerator and a denominator.
Only a **FRACTION** of people will get the joke.

What is a ballerina's favourite number?
**TWO-TWO.**

What kind of mistakes do ghosts make in maths?
**BOO-BOOS.**

Where did the **MATHS** teacher sit at lunch?
**At the times table.**

What kind of **PLIERS** do you use in arithmetic?
**Multipliers.**

What do you get if you add **25** and **917**, then subtract **765** and divide the answer by **33**?
**A headache.**
**(Unless you're Matilda!)**

What's a maths teacher's favourite lunch?
A **SQUARE** meal.

What do maths teachers eat at home?
**TAKEAWAYS.**

Which **TABLES** do you never have to learn in maths?
**DINNER** tables!

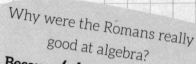

Why were the Romans really good at algebra?
**Because 'x' was always 10.**

What is a **FROG'S** favourite date?
**Any LEAP year.**

Why was the calendar so **ANXIOUS**?
**It knew its days were NUMBERED.**

Why did the girl take a tape measure to **BED**?
**She wanted to see how long she SLEPT.**

PARALLEL LINES have so much in common.

It's a shame they'll **NEVER MEET.**

Why do dogs run in **CIRCLES**?

It's hard to run in **SQUARES.**

$x^2$: Do you believe in God?

$x^3$: **Well, I do believe in higher powers . . .**

What would a tree say if it could talk?

**'GEOMETRY!'**

Why should you divide **TAN** by **SINE?** Just **COS.**

Why did the maths teacher lose his job? **He kept going off on a TANGENT.**

**MATHS JOKES . . .** are the first sine of **MADNESS.**

'The new maths teacher sets really hard tests, but it's OK because she's also incredibly mean.'
**'Why is that OK?'**
'Because two negatives make a positive!'

You know what seems **ODD** to me?
**Numbers that aren't divisible by 2.**

Why should you never talk to pi (π)?
**Because it always goes on FOREVER!**

What do you get when you cut an avocado into 6 x 71 x 19 pieces?
**GUACAMOLE.**

There are three kinds of pupil in this school.
**Those who are GOOD AT MATHS,** and those who aren't.

35

# SCIENCE
## Nature

Sometimes I think **ANIMALS** are cleverer than people. Cleverer than **SOME** people, certainly!

Animal jokes? **TOUCAN** play at that game.

What does a **DUCK** do with tricky homework? **Has a QUACK at it.**

Where do **POORLY PONIES** go? **The horsepital.**

What do **HEDGEHOGS** like on their sandwiches?

**Cheese and prickle.**

Where do **CLEVER CHICKENS** look for help with their homework?

**In the hencyclopaedia.**

What's green and wriggly and never shuts up?

**A chatterpillar.**

We don't have many **VEGETABLE** jokes yet.

**If you do, lettuce know.**

Why do **BIRDS FLY** south in the winter?

**Because it's too far to walk.**

What do you call a sleeping bull?

**A BULLDOZER.**

Which are the **STRONGEST** creatures in the sea?

**Mussels.**

Where can you weigh a **WHALE**?

**At a whale-weigh station.**

Why are **FISH** so clever?

**They live in schools.**

What's smarter than a talking **PARROT**?

**A spelling bee.**

Which **VEGETABLE** needs a plumber?

**A leek.**

What did the buffalo say to his son when he left for university?

**'Bison.'**

What kind of nut has no shell?

**A doughnut.**

Why do bees have sticky hair?

**Because they use honeycombs.**

Where do beavers keep their money?

**In the RIVER BANK.**

'What do you call the outside of a tree?'

**'I don't know.'**

'Bark.'

**'Woof, woof!'**

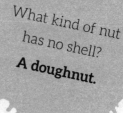

What do giraffes have that no other animals have?

**Baby giraffes.**

Why do **GIRAFFES** have such long necks?

**They can't stand the smell of their FEET.**

What's worse than knitting a **SCARF** for a **GIRAFFE**?

**Knitting SOCKS for a CENTIPEDE.**

# Electricity and physics

Some of these physics jokes are **SHOCKINGLY** good!

What's small, round, wrinkled and runs on **BATTERIES**?

**An electric currant.**

Why was the free **ELECTRON** sad?

**It had nothing to be positive about.**

'Miss, miss, help! I've lost an electron!'

**'Are you sure?'**

'Yes, I'm positive!'

How did Benjamin Franklin feel after discovering **ELECTRICITY**?

**Shocked.**

Which cake gives you an **ELECTRIC SHOCK**? A current bun.

What did Thomas Edison's mum say to him the night after he invented the **LIGHT BULB**? 'I'm really proud of you, but now turn it off and go to bed!'

'I just got struck by lightning!' **'How do you feel?'** 'SHOCKING!'

Why do **FLUORESCENT** lights hum?

**They forget the words.**

What did the mummy **LIGHT BULB** say to the baby light bulb?

'I love you watts and watts!'

A **PHOTON** checks into a hotel. 'Any luggage?' asks the receptionist.

'No, I'm travelling **LIGHT**.'

How much do the different parts of an **ATOM** cost?

Electrons and protons are one each, neutrons are **FREE** of **CHARGE**.

Where does bad **LIGHT** end up?

In a prism.

Who's on the case when the **ELECTRICITY** goes out?

Sherlock Ohms.

# Experiments

This book is like a **LABORATORY** for jokes. Get experimenting!

What did one **MAGNET** say to the other?

**'I find you very attractive.'**

Did you hear that oxygen and magnesium got together?

**OMg!**

Why did the **GERM** cross the microscope?

**To get to the other slide.**

I told a chemistry joke to a **NOBLE GAS.**

There was no reaction.

'Miss, miss, this lab smells of rotten eggs.'
**'Sorry to hear you're sulphuring.'**

The teacher threw **SODIUM CHLORIDE** at me.
**That's a salt!**

What's the difference between chemistry class and **COOKING**?
**In chemistry, you never lick the spoon.**

I blew up my chemistry experiment.
**Oxidants happen.**

What's a science teacher's favourite dog? **A LAB.**

What do you do with a **SICK** chemistry teacher? If you can't **HELIUM**, and you can't **CURIUM**, you might as well **BARIUM**.

I really love **CHEMISTRY**.
I'm in my element!

'Why have you drawn a wooden desk for this experiment?' **'Well, miss, you told us to draw what we see under the microscope.'**

Did you hear that oxygen and potassium went on a date?
**It went OK.**

I could make another **CHEMISTRY** joke. But all the good ones **ARGON**.

I don't trust **ATOMS**. I heard they make up everything.

What did the teacher say to her naughty science class? **'I've got my ION you.'**

# BOOK TITLES

**ELECTRICAL FAULTS** by Lou Swires

**The End of School** by Wendy Belgo

A
Frog's
Life

by
Lily Pond

**Telling Fibs** by Eliza Lott

Feeling Sick by Henrietta Maggott

I've never seen these books in my library before!

Alien Weapons by Ray Gunn

Blowing **Hot** and **Cold**
by
**Luke Warm**

**Sent Off**
by
Esau
Red

*Parachuting for Beginners*
by Hugo First

When Shall We Meet Again? by Miles Apart

# Space

Our nearest star is 4.24 light years away. I'd like to throw **MISS TRUNCHBULL** that far up into the solar system.

When do astronauts eat sandwiches? **LAUNCH TIME.**

How do you get a baby astronaut to sleep? **Rocket.**

What did Mars say to Saturn?

'Give me a ring sometime.'

Where do astronauts keep their sandwiches?
**In their launch boxes.**

What do astronauts have on their **CAKES**?
**Mars-ipan.**

What do astronauts put on their **TOAST**?
**Mars-malade.**

How does the **MOON** cut his hair?
**E-CLIPSE** it.

How does the solar system keep its **TROUSERS** up?

**With an asteroid belt.**

What did one **SHOOTING STAR** say to another?

**'Pleased to METEOR.'**

How do you organize a space **PARTY**?

**Planet.**

What's an astronaut's favourite board game?

**MOON-OPOLY.**

# Dinosaurs

You think teachers are old, but **DINOSAURS** are so old, they're fossils!

Why did **DINOSAURS** eat raw meat?

They hadn't learned how to cook yet.

Which dinosaur is the noisiest **SLEEPER**?

A brontosnorus.

Why can't you hear a **PTERODACTYL** on the toilet?

**Because it has a silent 'p'.**

What does a triceratops sit on?

**Its TRICERABOTTOM.**

What happens if a dinosaur drives a car?

**Tyrannosaurus WRECKS.**

How do dinosaurs decorate their bathrooms?

**REPTILES.**

What came after the dinosaur?

**Its TAIL.**

What do you call a dinosaur with a very wide **VOCABULARY**?

**A thesaurus.**

Why did the dinosaur cross the road?
**The CHICKEN** hadn't evolved yet.

How do you ask a dinosaur over for supper?
**'TEA, REX?'**

Which is a dinosaur's least favourite reindeer?
**COMET.**

Can you name **TEN** dinosaurs in **TEN** seconds?
**EIGHT** iguanodons and **TWO** stegosauruses.

What do you call a **DINOSAUR** who never gives up?

**A try-try-tryceratops.**

Why did the apatosaurus devour the **FACTORY**?

**She was a plant eater.**

Which was the **SCARIEST** prehistoric animal of them all?

**The terror-dactyl.**

Why did the archaeopteryx always catch the **WORM**?

**It was an EARLY BIRD.**

How did dinosaurs pass their **EXAMS**?

**With extinction.**

What do you call a dinosaur that's not very clever?

**A DOPE-LODOCUS.**

What do you call a **DINOSAUR** who hates being late?

**A pronto-saurus.**

What do you call a dinosaur who runs the **RODEO**?

**A bronco-saurus.**

# HISTORY
## General

I wish the Trunchbull was history . . .

What's the worst thing about **ANCIENT HISTORY** at school?
The teacher tends to Babylon.

What is a snake's favourite subject?
**HISSSTORY.**

Why is history the **FRUITIEST** subject in school?
Because it's full of dates.

'Why is your test score so low in history?'
**'You keep asking about things that happened before I was born!'**

What do Alexander the Great and **KERMIT THE FROG** have in common?

**Their middle name.**

Why are the early days of history called the **DARK AGES**?

**Because there were so many knights.**

Who **STOLE** from the rich to pay for the bows in his hair?

**Ribbon Hood.**

Where did **NAPOLEON** keep his armies?

**Up his SLEEVIES.**

# Pre-history and ancient history

Who was the **FASTEST** human in history?
**Adam – he was first in the human race.**

Who invented **FIRE**?
**Some bright spark.**

Who designed Noah's **ARK**?
**An ark-itect.**

How did **NOAH** see where he was going?
**Floodlights.**

How does Moses make **TEA** in the desert?

**Hebrews it.**

Why did the textbook keep moving around the classroom?

**It was Roman history.**

Did you hear about the really, really old potatoes?

**They were fried in Ancient Greece.**

Why did Julius Caesar need crayons?

**He wanted to Mark Antony.**

What did Hercules say to Cerberus? **'HELLO, HELLO, HELLO.'**

How was the Roman Empire split in half? **With a pair of CAESARS.**

Why did the **ROMANS** build straight roads? **So their soldiers didn't go round the bend.**

CAESAR: What's the weather today?
BRUTUS: **Hail, Caesar.**

Which **PHARAOH** played the trumpet?

**Tooting-khamun.**

Which **FRUIT** launched a thousand ships?

**Melon of Troy.**

Who was the biggest **ROBBER** in history?

**Atlas. He held up the whole world.**

Who refereed a **TENNIS** match between Caligula and Nero?

**A Roman Umpire.**

Where would you find **HADRIAN'S WALL**?

**At the bottom of Hadrian's garden.**

Which Roman emperor suffered from **HAYFEVER**?

Julius Sneezer.

How do you use an ancient Egyptian **DOORBELL**?

Toot and come in.

How can you tell when a **MUMMY** is angry?

He flips his lid.

# BOOK TITLES

THE RUNAWAY BULL   by Gay Topen

A Flaw in the Law   by Lou Pole

Secret Police   by Laura Norder

Robots

from

Outer

Space

by

Ann

Droid

Off

a

Cliff

by

Eileen

Dover

Sometimes you **CAN** judge a book by its cover, or at least its **TITLE** . . .

A Hole in My Bucket by Lee King

Great Mysteries by Hugh Dunnit

Without Warning by Oliver Sudden

CHAOS by May Hem

Desperation by Fran Tic

This Land is My Land by Terry Tory

# Kings, queens and knights

Where was Richard III **CROWNED**?

On his head.

What was James II's first act when he came to the throne?

**Sitting down.**

When a knight was killed in battle, what was written on his grave?

**Rust in peace.**

Why was King Arthur's court so tired?

He had a lot of **SLEEPLESS** knights.

Did King Arthur ever have bad dreams? **Yes, KNIGHTMARES.**

Who made King Arthur's round table? **Sir CUMFERENCE.**

Where did knights park their camels? **Camelot.**

Why did **HENRY VIII** have so many wives? **He liked to chop and change.**

Why is **BRITAIN** the wettest country?

Because the queen has reigned there for years.

Which queen scored the **BEST GOALS**?

Anne, because she got the Boleyn.

When did **QUEEN VICTORIA** die?

Just a few days before they buried her.

# World history

Which bus crossed the Atlantic Ocean?

**Christopher ColumBUS.**

Where was the Declaration of Independence signed?

**At the bottom.**

**WHY** did Columbus cross the ocean?

**To get to the other tide.**

What did they do at the **BOSTON TEA PARTY**?

**I don't know, I wasn't invited!**

Who succeeded the first **PRESIDENT** of the United States?

**The second one.**

Why did American Indians **HUNT** bear?

**They didn't, they wore clothes.**

How did the **VIKINGS** send secret messages?

**Norse code.**

Where do all the **PENCILS** come from?

**PENNSYLVANIA.**

What does the **STATUE OF LIBERTY** stand for?

She can't sit down.

Why did **CAPTAIN COOK** sail to Australia?

It was too far to swim.

If April showers bring **MAY FLOWERS**, what do May flowers bring?

Pilgrims.

# LUNCHTIME

All clever kids know that **LUNCH** is the best time of day at school . . .

'Miss, do you serve **LOBSTER?**'

'Hurry up and get a tray, child – we serve everyone.'

'Miss, miss, my plate's all wet!'

**'That's the SOUP, dear.'**

'Miss, miss, what's this fly doing in my soup?'

**'Looks like the BACKSTROKE.'**

Why are **DINNER LADIES** cruel?

Because they batter fish and beat eggs.

Why were the **STRAWBERRIES** upset?

They were in a **JAM.**

Did you hear the joke about the butter?

**DON'T SPREAD IT!**

Which fruit loves rollercoasters?

**A KI-WHEEEEE!**

What is the grumpiest apple?

**A CRABBY APPLE.**

Why is a **TOMATO** round and red?

Because if it was long and green, it would be a **CUCUMBER.**

How do you know carrots are good for your eyesight?

Have you ever seen a **RABBIT** wearing glasses?

What do you call a dropped pumpkin? **SQUASH.**

Why should you **NEVER** tell a secret in a cornfield? **There are too many ears around.**

Why did the cookie go to hospital? **It was feeling CRUMBY.**

What kind of snack swings from tree to tree? **A CHOCOLATE** chimp cookie.

Which vegetable goes best with jacket potatoes? **BUTTON MUSHROOMS.**

What's white, fluffy and **BEATS ITS CHEST** in the canteen? **A meringue-utang.**

What sits in custard and complains? **APPLE GRUMBLE.**

What's the biggest dessert in the world? **The Trifle Tower.**

What's the best way to see the Trifle Tower from above? **In a JELLYCOPTER.**

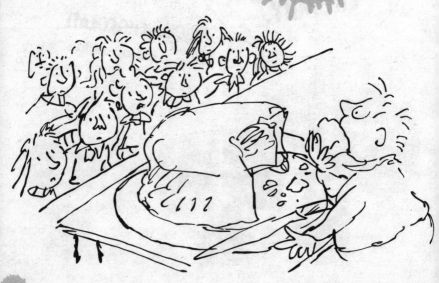

# Cook BOOKS

My dad **COOKED** the **BOOKS** at his garage, but here are some real cookbooks for you.

**Three Mice Tails** by A. Farmers-Wife

**Breakfast like a King** by Chris P. Bacon

**School Dinners** by Stew Pot

**QUICK SNACKS** by T.N. Biscuits

**Cooking Made Easy** by Mike Rowave

**School Dinner Basics** by Brendan Butter

**A Dog's Dinner** by Norah Bone

# BOOK TITLES

The Arctic Ocean by I. C. Waters

Serving in the ARMY by Reggie Ments

Information Brochures by Pam Fletts

Verse by Verse by Stan Za

THE FINAL WHISTLE by I. Blewit

A Guide to Undertaking by Paul Bearer

The Man Went Mad by E.B.A. Maniac

A SOLITARY LIFE by I. Malone

To Banbury Cross by Rhoda Whitehorse

Candlestick Jumping by Jack B. Nimble

# GEOGRAPHY

What's an ig?

An **INUIT'S HOME**
without a loo.

Why do the
**FRENCH**
eat snails?

They don't like
fast food.

Matilda
travelled all over
the **WORLD** while
sitting in her little
room in an English
village.

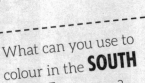

What can you use to
colour in the **SOUTH
POLE** on a map?

Felt-tipped penguins.

What's big, white, furry and always points **NORTH?**

**A polar bearing.**

Why does the **NORWEGIAN** navy put barcodes on the sides of their ships?

**So that, when they arrive at port, they can Scandinavian.**

How do you get **TWO WHALES** in a car?

**Down the M4 and across the Severn Bridge.**

How can you tell that compasses and scales are intelligent?

**They're all GRADUATED.**

What place is mentioned in this joke?

**THE BLACK SEA.**

Can anyone tell me what a volcano is?

What do **FISH AND MAPS** have in common?
**They both have scales.**

Where do **GHOSTS** go on holiday?
**The Dead Sea.**

What is the most impatient country?
**RUSSIA.**

What's green and 5,000 miles long?
**The Grape Wall of China.**

What do you call the little rivers that flow into the **NILE**?
**Juveniles.**

A mountain with hiccups.

Where are the Great Plains found?

At the **GREAT AIRPORTS.**

What's the **CAPITAL** of **France**?

**F.**

Which country gets the best night's sleep?

**Snore-way.**

What do you find in the middle of **EGYPT**?

**The letter 'y'.**

What was the largest island before **AUSTRALIA** was discovered?

**Australia.**

Which **CAT** always knows the right way to go?

**A com-puss.**

N

W    E

S

In Australia, what do they call a broken **BOOMERANG**?

**A stick.**

# MUSIC

Apparently, studying music makes you **CLEVERER.** These jokes certainly will.

Where do cultured **FROGS** go out in the evenings?

**THE HOPERA.**

What's a frog's **FAVOURITE** music?

**HIP-HOP.**

What kind of music do you find in outer **SPACE**?

Nep-tunes.

Why was the **MUSICIAN** arrested?

She was in treble.

What did the class send their **MUSIC TEACHER** when she was ill?

A get-well-soon **CHORD.**

Why couldn't the **STRING QUARTET** find their composer?

He was Haydn.

There are so many jokes about one particular **COMPOSER.**

I could make you a Liszt.

Why did the music teacher need a **LADDER**?

To reach the high notes.

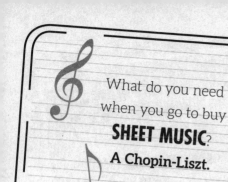

What do you need when you go to buy **SHEET MUSIC**? A Chopin-Liszt.

How does a **PRIMA DONNA** sing a scale?

Do, re, mi, me me me me ME!

Why do **PIRATES** always play opera on board?

**Because they love the high 'C's.**

'Music jokes are my forte.'

**'You could get in TREBLE with these funny jokes!'**

What note do you get if you drop a **PIANO** down a mineshaft?

**A flat minor.**

Give it a rest?

**Yeah, maybe that one fell FLAT.**

What happened to the sheet music criminal?

He got double time. Luckily the judge didn't have a **TEMPO**.

'Do you want to get **ICE CREAM** at the baroque music café?'

'No, thanks, I prefer Schubert.'

'Do you want more **MUSIC** jokes?'

'No, I don't think I can Handel it.'

# The orchestra

It's nice to play in the school orchestra – it drowns out the noise of the Trunchbull.

Which instrument do **SKELETONS** play?

The trombone.

Why do **BAGPIPERS** never run?
They could put an eye out or, worse, get kilt.

Why do bagpipers walk as they play?

To get away from the **NOISE.**

Which instrument do **MICE** play? **The MOUSE** organ.

Why was the **PIANO** outside the rehearsal-room door?

**Because it forgot its keys.**

Why are pianos the **POSHEST** instruments?

**Because they're either upright or grand.**

What's the difference between a **GUITAR** and a **FISH**?

**You can't tuna fish.**

What is the best instrument in the band?

**That's tricky, but the DRUM takes a lot of beating.**

How do you mend brass **INSTRUMENTS**?

With a tuba glue.

How do you make a **BANDSTAND**?

Take away their chairs.

Why didn't the **SKELETON** want to play in the school band?

His heart wasn't in it.

'Miss, miss, I've swallowed my **MOUTH ORGAN!**'

'Good thing you weren't playing the double bass.'

What happens when the school orchestra plays in a **THUNDERSTORM?**

The conductor gets hit by **LIGHTNING.**

How did the **PERCUSSIONIST** go fishing?

He took his cast-a-nets.

Why was the orchestra **BADLY BEHAVED** when their teacher was off sick?

They don't know how to conduct themselves.

# ART

Am I a phenomenon?

It is quite possible that you are.

Why did the girl take a **PENCIL** to bed?
**To draw the curtains.**

What did the pirate win at Prize Day?
**The ARRRRRRRT Prize.**

Why did **VAN GOGH** become a painter?
**Because he didn't have an EAR for music.**

What did **MICHELANGELO** say to the ceiling? **'I got you covered.'**

Why did the **PAINTBRUSH** go to the doctor? **It had a stroke.**

Where does a cow hang his paintings? **In a MOOOOSEUM.**

Did you hear about the artist who paints in **JAIL**? **He had a brush with the law.**

Why did he go to jail? **Because he'd been FRAMED.**

A man visits a museum. Suddenly he stops and says to the guide: 'Argh, it's ugly!'

**'I beg your pardon – that's a Picasso,' the guide answers.**

Further on, the man exclaims again: 'Argh, it's really ugly!'

**'That, sir, is a mirror!'**

How does Salvador Dalí start his mornings?

**With a bowl of SURREAL.**

Which painting is never happy?

**The MOANING Lisa.**

What do you call someone hanging on a wall?

**ART.**

Knock, knock.
**Who's there?**
Monet.
**Monet who?**
Monet doesn't
grow on trees.

What do you call a
painting by a cat?
**A PAW-TRAIT.**

Why did the bald man paint
rabbits on his head?
**Because from a distance they
looked like HARES!**

What's the most
artistic animal
on a farm?
**PABLO PIGASSO.**

Why did the art teacher praise **DRACULA**?

He was good at drawing **BLOOD**.

What's the second most **ARTISTIC ANIMAL** on a farm?

Vincent Van Goat.

Why were the **BLUE**, **PURPLE** and **ORANGE** paints being super-nice to each other?

They were all complimentary colours.

What's **GREEN** and smells like **BLUE** paint?

Green paint.

How do you beat an artist in a **RACE**?

**EASEL-Y.**

What is an artist's favourite swimming technique?

**BRUSHSTROKE.**

Did you hear about the **INDECISIVE ARTIST** who always took jokes too far?

**She didn't know where to draw the line.**

# RIDDLES FOR BREAK TIME

These riddles are for **SERIOUSLY** clever kids only. Can you work them out?

When is a **DOOR** not a door?
When it's **AJAR**.

What gets **WET** as it **DRIES**?
A towel.

What goes up as the **RAIN** comes down?
An **UMBRELLA**.

What have **HEADS AND TAILS** but no bodies?
**COINS**.

What goes **UP** but never comes **DOWN**? Your **AGE**.

What can you hold but **NEVER TOUCH**? Your breath.

What has a **BOTTOM** at its top? **A LEG.**

Which **ANIMAL** can jump higher than a house?

Any animal – houses can't **JUMP.**

How many children can you fit in an **EMPTY** classroom?

**One! After that it's not empty.**

What can **TRAVEL THE WORLD** but stay in one corner?

**A STAMP.**

What always runs but **NEVER WALKS**, often murmurs but **NEVER SPEAKS**, has a bed but **NEVER SLEEPS** and has a mouth but **NEVER TALKS**?

A river.

What does everybody get at every single **BIRTHDAY**?

One year older.

**THREE SAILORS** fell out of a boat, but only two got their hair wet. Why?

**The third sailor was bald.**

What's the difference between **SEE AND SEA**? You can see the sea, but the sea cannot see you.

What word, when pronounced **RIGHT IS WRONG**, but if pronounced wrong is right? 'Wrong.' **RIGHT!**

What's the difference between a butcher and an **INSOMNIAC**? One weighs a steak and the other stays **AWAKE.**

What's the difference between someone desperate for the loo and someone trapped in a lion enclosure at the **ZOO**?

**One is dying to go and the other is going to die.**

What's the difference between a **MUSICIAN** and a **CORPSE**?

**One composes, the other DECOMPOSES.**

What's the difference between a **WIZARD** and the letters 'a', 'e', 'k', 'm' and 's'?

**One makes SPELLS and the other spells 'makes'.**

# P.E.

The Trunchbull might be a stupid headmistress but she was good enough at the hammer to throw in the **OLYMPICS**. With these jokes you could get a gold medal in being funny!

How do **ORANGES** play cricket?

**With fruit bats.**

What do you call a boy floating in the swimming pool?

**BOB.**

'Did you hear about the **TWO VAMPIRES** in the 100m race?'

'Yes, it was neck and neck.'

How do you start a **LIGHT-BULB** race?

'Ready, steady, glow.'

A tap, a **LETTUCE** and a **TOMATO** were in the 100m final. What happened?

The tap was running, the lettuce was ahead and the tomato was trying to **KETCHUP**.

Why are fish rubbish at **TENNIS**? They don't like getting close to the net.

Why did the
**CRICKET TEAM** invite
the **DINNER LADIES**
to play?

**They needed
a good batter.**

What's a
**LIZARD'S**
favourite sport?

**Cricket.**

How can you **SWIM** one
mile in just a few seconds?
**Go over a WATERFALL.**

Why did the raisin win
all the races at the
**SWIMMING GALA?**
**It was a strong currant.**

Which is the
**WARMEST**
athlete?
**The long
jumper.**

What happens if you play **TABLE TENNIS** with a bad egg?

First it goes ping, then it goes **PONG.**

What happened when **TWO BALLS** of string had a race?

It ended in a tie.

'Do you want to try **ROCK CLIMBING**?'

'I would if I were boulder.'

What lights up a **FOOTBALL** stadium?

A football match.

What happened when two **WAVES** had a race?

They **TIDE.**

# LANGUAGES

We learn **FRENCH** at school. What other languages do you know?

Why do French people never order two **EGGS** for breakfast?
**Because one egg is un oeuf.**

Don't eat the **FRENCH FISH**! It's **POISSON.**

Why did the **FRENCH CHICKEN** cross the road in a bikini?
**To get to the swimming POULE.**

Did you hear about the **FRENCH TEACHER** who fell off a roof into a pile of baguettes?

**She was in a lot of pain.**

In **PARIS**, what do they call a really bad Thursday?

**A tra-jeudi.**

What happens if you invite six other French people over for **DINNER**?

**They sept the table.**

What happened to the last **FIVE FRENCH SHIPS** in a storm?

**They cinq.**

In the Cat Olympics swimming final there was an American cat called **ONE TWO THREE**, a French cat called **UN DEUX TROIS** and a German cat called **EIN ZWEI DREI**. The American cat finished first, the German cat finished second, but the French cat was nowhere to be seen.
Because **UN DEUX TROIS QUATRE CINQ**.

No matter how **KIND** you are...
German children will always be **KINDER**.

A schoolboy was scared of **GERMAN SAUSAGES**.

He feared the **WURST**.

What do you call a French boy wearing **SANDALS**?
Phillipe Phillope.

In **SPAIN**, what does the sun dance to?

**Sol music.**

How does **SPANISH MILK** introduce itself?

**Soy milk!**

Where does **PEPPERONI** go on holiday?

**The Leaning Tower of PIZZA.**

How does a **MATADOR** take his coffee in France?

**AU LAIT!**

'Miss, miss, I'm going to a **FANCY-DRESS PARTY** as an Italian island!'

**'Don't be Sicily.'**

What do you call fake **SPAGHETTI**?

**An IMPASTA.**

# I.T.

Is there a Trunchbull in your school? If you're clever, you could hide in the computer lab – behind a screensaver!

Why was the **COMPUTER** cold?

It left its Windows open.

How do **HEAD LICE** email each other?

Over the internit.

Why did the computer **SQUEAK**?

Somebody stepped on its **MOUSE**.

How do **SQUIRRELS** send emails?

On the **INTERNUT.**

What did the **SPIDER** do in the computer lesson?

Made a **WEBSITE.**

What do computers do at **LUNCHTIME**?

Have a byte.

What do you get if you cross a **COMPUTER** and a **LIFEGUARD**?

A screensaver.

What is a computer's favourite snack?

**MICROCHIPS.**

Why did the computer **SNEEZE**?

It had a virus.

Why can't computers play **TENNIS**?

**They try to surf the net.**

How does a **CAT** stop a video file?

**It presses PAWS.**

What do you get if you cross a **COMPUTER** with an **ELEPHANT**?

**Lots of MEMORY.**

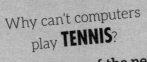

Which is the **BEST WEBSITE** in the savannah?

**The Onlion King.**

How does a tree get its **EMAIL**?

**It logs on.**

In which European city do people receive the most **UNWANTED EMAILS**?

**Spamsterdam.**

Two dozen **COMPUTER SCREENS** were stolen from the school last night.

**The police are monitoring the situation.**

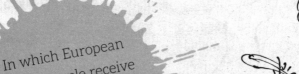

# DRAMA

It's the only lesson where you are meant to make a scene!

Did you hear about the **DRAMA-CLUB** pupils who fell through the floor?

**It was just a stage they were going through.**

How many **DANCERS** does it take to change a light bulb?

**Five, six, seven, eight!**

What do you call a performing **CHICKEN**?

**A hentertainer.**

# HOME TIME

Even clever kids need to let off steam. Here are some seriously **SILLY JOKES** for home time!

Why was the biscuit **HOMESICK**?

She'd been a **WAFER** so long.

Did you hear about the **BALLOON** family with one **NAUGHTY** child?

He let them all down.

What do ghosts call their **PARENTS**?

Transparents.

'What are you doing at the **CINEMA**?'

'Well, I really liked the **BOOK**'.

How does a **CHICKEN** cross a busy road?

**It says, 'Eggs-cuse me!'**

At the **CINEMA**, a child sees a penguin sitting next to him. 'Are you really a penguin?'

**'Yes.'**

What do you call a mischievous **EGG**?

**A practical yolker.**

Which **CHICKENS** tell the best jokes?

**Comedi-hens.**

What do you call two **WITCHES** living together?

**Broom-mates.**

Has anyone ever seen the **ABOMINABLE** Snowman?

**Not yeti.**

What do you do if you find a **SNAKE** in your loo?

**Wait till it's finished.**

What do you get if you cross **TWO SNAKES** with a magic spell?

**ADDERCADABRA** and **ABRADACOBRA.**

I usually charge for my **CHIMNEY JOKES.**

**This one's on the house.**

What bird steals the **SOAP** from your **BATH**?

**A robber duck.**

What goes **'DOT-DOT-CROAK, DOT-DASH-CROAK'**?

**Morse toad.**

What goes
**'DOT-DOT-SQUEAK,
DOT-DASH-SQUEAK'**?

Mouse code.

What do **ANGRY RODENTS**
send each other in December?
**CROSS**-mouse cards.

Why was the
**INSECT** asked to
leave the park?

It was a
**LITTERBUG.**

When did the fly fly?
**When the SPIDER**
spied her.

127

# MISS TRUNCHBULL'S INSULTS!

That's not **FUNNY**, you ...

Stop **LAUGHING**, you ...

You're not so **CLEVER**, you ...

**STOP** laughing or it's the Chokey for you, you ...

**GIGGLING** children will be sent to the **CHOKEY**!

How **DARE** you **LAUGH**, you ...

Please be careful putting this book away. Last week a book fell on Miss Trunchbull's head – and she had only her shelf to blame.

# ROALD DAHL

was a spy, ace fighter pilot, chocolate
historian and medical inventor.
He was also the author of *Charlie and the
Chocolate Factory*, *Matilda*, *The BFG* and many
more brilliant stories. He remains
## THE WORLD'S NUMBER ONE STORYTELLER.

# QUENTIN BLAKE

has illustrated more than three hundred books
and was Roald Dahl's favourite illustrator.
In 1980 he won the prestigious
Kate Greenaway Medal. In 1999 he became
the first ever Children's Laureate and in 2013
he was knighted for services to illustration.

# HOW MANY HAVE YOU READ?

## FEWER THAN 5?

### WHOOPSY-SPLUNKERS!

You've got some reading to do!

# Between 5 and 10?
Wonderful surprises await!
Keep reading . . .

# More than 10?
Whoopee!
Which was your favourite?

FANTASTIC
PHIZZ-WHIZZING
BOOKS
INSPIRED BY
ROALD DAHL'S
WORLD...

# ROALD DAHL DAY

## CELEBRATE

### THE PHIZZ-WHIZZING WORLD of ROALD DAHL

### EVERY YEAR on

# 13th SEPTEMBER!